C000181080

Text: Vivienne Crow

Photographs: Vivienne Crow, Carl Rogers, Shutterstock, Dreamstime, Stewart Smith Photography, Tony Bowerman, Jonathan Ward, Paul King, Steve Thompson

Design: Carl Rogers

Important Advice: The routes described in this book are undertaken at the reader's own risk. Walkers should take into account their level of fitness, wear suitable footwear and clothing, and carry food and water. It is also advisable to take the relevant OS map with you in case you get lost and leave the area covered by our maps.

Whilst every care has been taken to ensure the accuracy of the route directions, the publishers cannot accept responsibility for errors or omissions, or for changes in the details given. Nor can the publisher and copyright owners accept responsibility for any consequences arising from the use of this book.

If you find any inaccuracies in either the text or maps, please either write to us or email us at the addresses below. Thank you.

n Northern
E Eye

Northern Eye Books
ISBN 978-1-908632-00-5

A CIP catalogue record for this book is available from the British Library

www.northerneyebooks.co.uk

First published in 2012 by

Northern Eye Books Limited
Tattenhall, Cheshire CH3 9PX

Email: tony@northerneyebooks.com

For sales enquiries, please call 01928 723 /44

Cover: *Lakeland waterfall by Stewart Smith*
(www.stewartsmithphotography.co.uk)

Contents

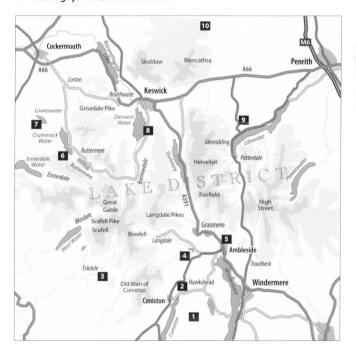

England's Largest National Park

THE LAKE DISTRICT NATIONAL PARK is the largest and most popular of the thirteen National Parks in England and Wales. Created as one of Britain's first National Parks in 1951, its role is to 'conserve and enhance' the natural beauty, wildlife and culture of this iconic English landscape, not just for residents and visitors today but for future generations, too.

Remarkably, the National Park contains every scrap of England's land over 3,000 feet, including its highest mountain, Scafell Pike. Packed within the Park's 885 square miles are numerous peaks and fells, over 400 lakes and tarns, around 50 dales, six National Nature Reserves, and more than 100 Sites of Special Scientific Interest—all publicly accessible on over 1,800 miles of footpaths and other rights of way. It's no surprise then, that the Lake District attracts an estimated 15 million visitors a year.

Lake District Waterfalls

The dramatic waterfalls of the Lake District are mostly a by-product of the last Ice Age—the awesome result of the ancient interplay of ice and rock. Given perpetual life by the region's high rainfall, they come thundering down from the fells in a variety of forms. No two are the same.

Many carry the name 'force'—from the old Norse *foss* simply meaning 'waterfall'—a remnant of the times when Norsemen dominated these uplands.

"The white downfall…glimmered through the trees, that hang before it like the bushy hair over a madman's eyes."

Samuel Taylor Coleridge on Scale Force (1802)

TOP 10 **Walks:** Walks to Waterfalls

THERE ARE COUNTLESS WATERFALLS all over the Lake District: from gentle becks cascading down from the fells to noisy, tumultuous surges of foaming whitewater and elegant ribbons plummeting over the edge of sheer rock faces. The ten featured here are some of the highest and most impressive in the National Park. Some are hidden away in dark, atmospheric gorges, others are set in pretty woodland. But each of them will leave you exhilarated by their drama and their power.

Force Falls — page 8

Tom Gill — page 12

Stanley Ghyll Force — page 18

Skelwith & Colwith Forces — page 24

Force Falls is made up of a series of cascades

Force Falls

A chance to see wildlife, sculptures and a powerful waterfall on a wander through Grizedale Forest

What to expect:
Forest tracks and paths; some road walking; muddy in places

Distance/time: 9.5km/ 6 miles. Allow 2½-3 hours

Start: Forestry Commission car park at Blind Lane near Force Mills, about 2½ miles south of the Grizedale Forest Visitor Centre

Grid ref: SD 344 912

Ordnance Survey Map: OL 7 *The English Lakes South-eastern area Windermere, Kendal and Silverdale*

After the walk: The Eagle's Head pub, Satterthwaite

Walk outline

This walk explores the pretty mixed woodland on the southern edge of Grizedale Forest. A series of forest tracks and trails leads down to the quiet village of Satterthwaite. After a short section of road walking, the route then re-enters the woods, passing one of Grizedale's famous sculptures, and eventually loops back up to Force Falls.

Force Falls

At the southern end of Grizedale Forest, the valley's main beck comes crashing down through the woods in a steep series of white-water cascades. The tremendous force of the water was once used to power corn and bobbin mills at Force Mill, built in 1694 and still standing at the base of the falls. It also powered a bloomery forge, used in the local iron-making industry until smelt furnaces were built further south.

Satterthwaite church

As well as housing a famous sculpture trail, Grizedale Forest is home to a few Lake District rarities, including dormice, the elusive pine marten and the recently re-introduced red kite.

Dormouse

The Walk

1. With your back to the road, follow the trail up to the right. Keep to the green and white waymarked route and then turn left along a forest road. On reaching a sharp, right-hand bend in the track—with another, grassy track to the left—go straight across to pick up a narrow trail through the trees. This eventually becomes a surfaced lane as it enters **Satterthwaite village**.

2. At the church, turn left along the road and, just beyond **Satterthwaite Bridge**, turn right up a rough track. In about 150 metres, bear left along a path marked by green-topped posts. At a faint fork, bear left, keeping to the waymarked trail.

3. Turn right at a wide forest track, soon passing a sculpture of two bathers below a **small waterfall**. The track swings left and climbs. Turn left at the junction and, in about 250 metres, bear left along an easy-to-miss path running just below the main track.

4. Turn right at a minor road and then, in 100 metres, go through a gap between the buildings on your left and swing right, through a large gate. Just before the next gate, bear left to cross **Force Beck** via a footbridge. Enter a coppice via a large gate and, after 50 metres, turn right along a track. After going through another tall gate, ignore one muddy track to the left and then bear left along a signposted trail and through a gap in the wall. At the top of a short climb, the path swings right. Bear left at a faint fork as you drop down the other side.

5. Turn left along a minor road near **Rusland church**. As you draw level with

Cold shower: *Wooden sculpture of bathers enjoying a refreshing dip in Grizedale Forest*

a road on your right, turn left. This rough track climbs with a wall on your left.

6. On reaching a road, turn right and then follow it round to the left, climbing alongside **Force Falls**. At the top of the waterfall, turn right—along a green and white waymarked trail. Bear right at a fork. About 70 metres after crossing a wall, bear right, crossing back over it. Descend through the trees to return to the car park. ♦

Red kites

Red kites were re-introduced to Cumbria in 2010, with the initial release of 30 young birds in Grizedale Forest. Following decades of persecution by farmers and gamekeepers, they had been lost from much of England and Scotland in the second half of the 19th century. These large but graceful birds of prey are unmistakeable in flight—with their deeply forked tails, long, angled wings and distinctive, reddish-brown colouring.

Tom Gill

Tom Gill

A straightforward stroll past waterfalls to a delightful beauty spot

Distance/time: 6km/ 3½ miles. Allow 2-2½ hours

Start: National Trust pay and display car park at Tom Gill on the A593, 2 miles north of Coniston

Grid ref: SD 321 999

Ordnance Survey Map: OL 7 *The English Lakes South-eastern area. Windermere, Kendal & Silverdale*

After the walk: Wide choice of pubs and cafés in Coniston

Walk outline

The climb through Glen Mary is relatively easy, passing the Tom Gill waterfalls on the way. Emerging from the trees, the next section is a partial circuit of Tarn Hows, one of Lakeland's most popular beauty spots. Leaving the crowds behind, we head back into the trees, joining an old byway, and then return via a quiet valley path to pretty Yew Tree Tarn.

Tom Gill

The waterfalls of Tom Gill sit in an attractive, wooded ravine to the west of Tarn Hows, forming the tarn's main outlet stream. As walkers climb gently through the trees, two sets of waterfalls are encountered. The first, small cascade is an impressive sight, but this is only a foretaste of what lies further upstream. As the path narrows and the gorge steepens and darkens, the slender, white plume of the main waterfall appears, plunging ten metres over the dark rocks. It's a modest affair by Lakeland standards, but well worth a visit. The culminating moment then comes as you leave the ravine and are greeted by Tarn Hows.

Yew Tree Tarn

Bluebells

Lily pond: *Water lilies sprinkle the mirrored surface of Tarn Hows in high summer*

The Walk

1. Take the path behind the information panels in the car park, cross the bridge and turn right—signposted to 'Tarn Hows'. A lovely path heads gently uphill through the mostly deciduous woodland beside **Tom Gill**. As it bends left, you catch a glimpse of the first cascades.

Continuing through the trees, you reach a signpost indicating the way to the main waterfall. This path has steep,

unfenced drops on one side, so watch your footing, and keep a close eye on young children and dogs. The main waterfall is soon visible through the trees. The path climbs alongside it and then goes through a kissing-gate at the top, before edging closer to the noisy, tumultuous beck.

2. Finally, the drama is over and you reach a wide path at the edge of peaceful but popular **Tarn Hows**. Turn right and then, after the gate, bear left at the three-way split in the path. This keeps close to the tarn at first but then, climbing away from the water slightly, joins another path coming in from the right. Keep ahead through the next gate, enjoying views over the tarn. At a fork, keep right, along the higher path.

There used to be three tiny tarns here, but the single body of water you see today was created when the 19th-century industrialist James Marshall dammed one of them. With plans based on ideas of the 'Picturesque' that were popular at the time, he wanted to create something beautiful. To the west, Wetherlam and the Coniston fells provide a craggy backdrop to the delightful scene.

You will notice that, although it is dominated by conifers, there are a wide variety of trees around Tarn Hows. These were planted by James Marshall. He planted sycamore, beech and cherry trees on dry ground and alder and willow in wetter places with Scots pine, spruce and birch on the knolls. The woodland on this north-eastern side of the tarn is known as Rose Castle Plantation, and has several large redwoods in it, planted by James' son Victor.

The path drops back down to tarn level, crosses a bridge and goes through a gate.

3. Make sure you are not distracted by the faint orienteering trails heading off into the trees, but then turn right at the next obvious path junction—signposted 'Langdales and Arnside'.

4. A kissing-gate leads on to a rough track, along which you turn left. Peaceful as it may seem most of the time, there is a chance of encountering off-road vehicles on this track. Eventually, you drop to a surfaced lane, along which you bear left.

0		1km
	½ mile	

Morning calm: *A view across Holme Fell to snow-flecked Wetherlam*

5. On reaching the main road, cross straight over, making for the narrow lane on the other side. Immediately turn left, through the kissing-gate. The path now runs parallel with the road, along the base of **Holme Fell** up to the right. Just over a kilometre after joining the path—and having passed a couple of gates providing access to the road on your left—you pass through a gate and walk beside a beck.

6. On reaching a signpost in the woods in a short while, keep straight ahead (south-west) through the towering conifers. The signpost indicates that you are following the circuit of **Yew Tree Tarn**, but there isn't a path on the ground at this point. When you reach the wall, however, you pick up a good path that skirts the western edge of the tarn and then crosses the dam at its southern end.

Yew Tree Tarn was another of the Marshall family's creations. It was dammed by James Marshall's grandson Aubrey in 1923 as part of a trout fishery. In keeping with his grandfather's ideas about designed landscapes, he planted azaleas and conifers to 'add' to the natural beauty of the area.

7. Follow the path up to the right and, nearing the road, you will see a National Trust waymarker, indicating a faint trail beside the wall on the right. When this reaches the asphalt, carefully cross over to pick up a path heading right, through the trees. This runs parallel with the road and later recrosses the bridge over **Tom Gill** to return to the car park. ♦

The Gin Tree

You may spot the occasional juniper bush on the eastern slopes of Holme Fell. Reach out, squeeze one of the berries and sniff it. There's no mistaking which spirit it's used to flavour—gin. The Lake District used to be covered in huge forests of juniper, but much of it has gone now. Many old bushes are not being naturally replaced owing to shading from other plants and grazing pressures.

Stanley Ghyll Force

Stanley Ghyll Force

A meandering amble through gorgeous Eskdale, visiting a ribbon waterfall in a narrow, verdant ghyll

What to expect:

Woodland and riverside paths, one steep section; slippery rocks in gorge

---

Distance/time: 7km/ 4¼ miles. Allow 2-2½ hours

Start: Trough House Bridge car park near Dalegarth Hall. It's around 350 metres down an unmarked lane off the road through Eskdale

Grid ref: NY 171 002

Ordnance Survey Map: OL 6 *The English Lakes South-western area. Coniston, Ulverston & Barrow-in-Furness*

After the walk: The Boot Inn and the Brook House Inn in Boot; or Fellbites Café at nearby Dalegarth Station

---

Walk outline

This mostly gentle stroll forms a figure of eight, with Stanley Ghyll making up the first loop. The second, longer loop follows a bridleway in and out of woodland as far as Doctor Bridge and then returns along a beautiful riverside path. The only difficulty comes at the top of Stanley Ghyll where the rocky path becomes slippery, but this section can be missed out.

Stanley Ghyll Force

Eskdale's Stanley Ghyll Force is located in a dark but lush world that is quite unlike anything else in the Lake District. The steep sides of the gorge are dripping with mosses and ferns, some of which are rare; and, even when the outside world is cool, you can feel the humidity rising. As you make your way upstream, crossing and recrossing the beck, this narrow trench slowly closes in around you. Finally, as you carefully negotiate the last rocky section of path, this splendid eighteen-metre sliver of white water is revealed, gushing down through a hidden gap in the almost black rock.

Walking up the beck

Lesser celandines

The Walk

1. Leave the car park and turn left. Keep left when the track to 'Dalegarth Hall' heads right. Take note as you pass a bridleway on the left after the next gate; you will return to this spot to start the second loop of the walk later. Just as the track swings right and starts to climb, go through the gate on the left—signposted 'To the waterfalls'. A clear path heads upstream through a beautiful area of mixed woodland.

After crossing the second railed bridge, you climb a flight of steps. At the top, the main route heads right, but if you want to see **Stanley Ghyll Force**, continue upstream to cross the third and final bridge.

Confident walkers will probably ignore the signs warning of the steep, slippery path ahead and continue along the side of the cliff to see the waterfall in all its glory. But if the soles of your boots aren't up to tackling damp rock, it's best to stop at the bridge.

2. Back on the main route, climb out of the gorge on a switch-back path just above the steps after the second bridge. It climbs fairly gently at first and then reaches a tiny bridge. Don't cross this; instead, follow the path up to the right, climbing more steeply. Just before it starts to drop, turn left along a narrow trail. Go through the gate and continue in the same direction. You quickly come to a track along which you turn right.

3. Soon after passing the gate, on your right, through which you entered

© Crown copyright and/or database right. All rights reserved. License number 100047867

Across the water: *Doctor Bridge on the River Esk on a sunny summer's day*

Stanley Ghyll, turn right through the waymarked gate you saw earlier—signposted 'Boot and Upper Eskdale'. Cross the narrow bridge over **Birker Beck**. After the next gate, bear right, following the line of the wall/fence on your right for about 30 metres and then swing left, along a grassy swathe through the bracken and gorse.

Having crossed a small ford, ignore the signposted bridleway going through the gap in the wall; instead, swing right and then immediately left to keep the wall on your left. Keep left at a fork, as indicated by the waymarker. Having gone through one area of woodland, with the **River Esk** below, keep following the wall. Ignore a grassy path to the right when you reach **Low Birker**; simply follow the track down in front of the farm.

4. Cross the stone, humpback bridge—known as **Doctor Bridge**—and turn left along a pleasant riverside path. You follow the river for a short while and then, when the path splits, keep left,

Secret world: *Birker Beck runs through a dark, steep-sided gorge in Eskdale*

walking with a wall on your left. If you look across the river now, you will see **Birker Force** punching its way through a gap in the crags on the southern side of the valley. Drawing level with the western end of these crags, go through a gate. The wall on your left now swings down towards the river. Leaving the main path here, stick with the wall and drop near to a **bridge over the Esk**. Don't cross it though; turn right to continue downstream to **St Catherine's Church**.

St Catherine's forms the southern terminus of the old Wasdale to Eskdale corpse road. Before St Olaf's Church at Wasdale Head was licensed for burials, coffins had to be carried on horseback to St Catherine's. Needless to say, there are plenty of spooky stories associated with it...

On one stormy winter's day, it is said, the horse carrying the coffin of a young local man suddenly took fright and disappeared on Eskdale Moor. When the dead man's elderly mother heard that her son's body had been lost, the shock proved too much for her and she died. A coffin was again strapped to the back of a horse and the party set off. Again, the group experienced

bad weather and, again, the horse bolted. It was never seen again, although people say you can sometimes hear hoofbeats on the moor when the fog descends.

5. At the church, turn right along a lane and then left along an unmarked path between drystone walls. After a gate, turn left along the quiet lane. The car park is on your left, about 100 metres after **Trough House Bridge**. ♦

Cumbria's Little Ratty

Eskdale is home to the narrow gauge Ravenglass and Eskdale Railway, also known affectionately as the La'al Ratty. It first opened in 1875 to carry iron ore from the mine at Boot to the main railway line at Drigg. Today, using miniature steam engines and tiny carriages, the 15 inch-gauge line carries tourists through beautiful Lake District scenery—from Ravenglass on the Irish Sea coast to Dalegarth near Boot.

Skelwith Force

Skelwith & Colwith Forces

A rhapsodic ramble through woods and beside rivers, taking in two magnificent waterfalls

What to expect:
Good woodland and riverside paths and tracks; some quiet roads

Distance/time: 9km/ 5½ miles. Allow 2¾-3¼ hours

Start: National Trust pay and display car park in Elterwater village

Grid ref: NY 327 047

Ordnance Survey Map: OL 7 *The English Lakes South-eastern area. Windermere, Kendal & Silverdale*

After the walk: Britannia Inn, Elterwater

Walk outline

There's plenty to see on this walk, which starts with a peaceful riverside stroll leading to two very different, but very imposing waterfalls—Skelwith Force and Colwith Force. It then meanders through pretty woodland into Little Langdale where there's an opportunity to visit fascinating quarry workings before crossing Slater Bridge. The return route is mostly on tracks and quiet lanes.

Skelwith Force and Colwith Force

Skelwith Force is on the River Brathay, just upstream of Skelwith Bridge. It is, by Lakeland standards, a small waterfall—with a drop of less than five metres. But stand on the rocks beside it after heavy rain and your senses will undoubtedly be overwhelmed by the noise, the spray and the sight of this broad, furious river as it forces itself through a narrowing channel.

A short walk away, Colwith Force is another beast entirely. Although the falls are equally powerful and equally impressive, here the River Brathay suddenly plummets seventeen metres, cleft into two foaming torrents on its violent descent.

Skelwith Bridge

Grey wagtail

The Walk

1. Walk over to the wall beside the beck in the car park and then turn left, going through a gate to access a constructed riverside path. This later veers away from the water for a short while but then emerges close to **Elter Water**. Continue alongside the beck and through a gate to reach a bridge.

You will cross this in a short while, but, for now, follow the beckside path for a further 80 metres for a view of **Skelwith Force**.

2. After admiring the falls, walk back to the bridge. Cross it and continue along the clear path—with good views of the waterfall and the **River Brathay**. Soon after passing

a house on the left, join another path from the left. Leave the woods via a gate and, soon after this, join a rough track coming in from the left. After passing in front of **Park House**, head to the left of a tiny shed to pass through two gates in quick succession.

The path leads up to **Elterwater Park**. Swing left as you cross the yard to reach the access road. To continue along the path, cross diagonally to your right. The route crosses some stiles to reach another private road. Go straight over and through the gate to head downhill. More stiles and a section of riverside path lead to a minor road.

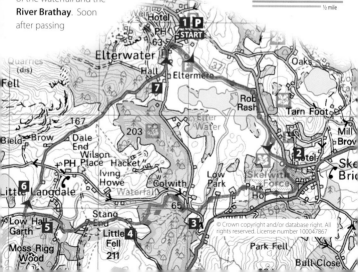

Twin falls: *The River Brathay makes a dramatic exit from Little Langdale at Colwith Force*

3. Turn right and walk along the asphalt for 80 metres. Now go up the slate steps on the left and through a gate. Bearing right, you soon have to clamber over some slippery rocks to gain the riverside route. As you head upstream, keeping to the path nearest the river, the sense of anticipation mounts as the beck becomes noisier and faster moving. On reaching a fork at the bottom of some steps, bear right for a short detour and a grand view of **Colwith Force**.

Once you've seen the falls, retrace your steps to the fork and then bear right to climb the steps. With a steep drop on your right, the path swings round for another view of the falls and then splits. Bear left, soon climbing through the woods. When you reach a junction with another path at the edge of the woods, bear right, through a gate. Follow the wall on your right for a few metres and then go through the gate.

4. When you reach **High Park**, go through another gate, turn right towards the farm and then swing left

Sound and fury: *The River Brathay plunges over Skelwith Force*

through the yard. Go through the large wooden gate on the left, opposite the barn, and then turn right along the lane. On reaching the next set of buildings at **Stang End**, bear right—towards 'Elterwater and Ambleside'. The lane crosses a small beck after which it becomes rougher underfoot. It then joins a track coming in from the left to drop to the **River Brathay** near a footbridge.

5. As you continue, you will pass the entrance to some disused quarries.

If you want to explore the workings, watch for a gated track to the left about 300 metres after the footbridge. Although the gate is locked, there is a stile beside it. The track climbs to a short tunnel that leads to the impressive cavern known as **Cathedral Quarry.** *It is possible to explore other tunnels and old workings from here, but bear in mind that you will need a torch and that there are dangers associated with these quarries.*

Continue along the main track until you see a kissing-gate in the wall on your right. Go through this and then cross **Slater Bridge**.

6. Keep left to climb gently with a wall

on your right. On reaching some farm buildings, bear left on a track that leads to the road. Turn left and immediately right on to a surfaced lane. This lane becomes rougher underfoot as you pass a farm. Keep following this track, ignoring any paths off to the left, for around a kilometre.

7. Keep straight on at a surfaced lane and then turn left at the road. The car park is now 300 metres on the right. ♦

Slater Bridge

This ancient, two-part bridge once gave workers access to the slate quarries, hence its name. But there are also suggestions that it may date back to Roman times, or that it was named after the Sleyther family in the late 14th century. Only wide enough to allow one person to cross at a time, the ancient bridge has had an iron railing added in more recent times.

Stockghyll Force

Stockghyll Force

A short walk to a popular waterfall, followed by a chance to explore the valley upstream

What to expect:
Woodland trails, quiet roads, farm paths and tracks

Distance/time: 4.5km/ 2¾ miles. Allow 1¾-2 hours

Start: Main car park in Ambleside, just north of the town centre on the A591

Grid ref: NY 375 047

Ordnance Survey Map: OL 7 *The English Lakes South-eastern area. Windermere, Kendal & Silverdale*

After the walk: Pubs, cafés and tearooms in Ambleside

Walk outline

This short walk climbs gently to the top of Stockghyll Force, making use of good paths and several superb viewpoints along the way. With views of the surrounding fells gradually opening out, it continues upstream along a quiet lane, crosses the beck and returns to Ambleside via farm paths, rough tracks and residential roads on the edge of the town.

Stockghyll Force

Stockghyll Force is an impressive waterfall hidden away in a colourful, wooded ravine just a stone's throw from the centre of busy Ambleside. The two main ribbons of water that make up these falls plunge between the moss-covered sides of the steep, rocky gorge, uniting to form one powerful channel on the way—and falling a total of twenty-seven metres in the process. There are plenty of places from which to view the falls, one of the most dramatic being the footbridge over the top of them—although you'll have to shout to make yourself heard over the tumult.

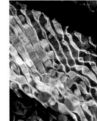

Sunlight in the shallows

Dipper

The Walk

1. Cross the pedestrian bridge from the car park on to the main road and turn right. Follow the road round to the left, soon passing the **Salutation Hotel** on the left. Turn left along a lane immediately after **Barclays Bank**, and then take the next lane on the left. You will see a sign pointing 'To the waterfalls' on the wall here.

The area around Stock Ghyll was once noisy with the sound of mills—wool fulling mills at first, later replaced by paper mills and bobbin-turning mills.

2. Follow this lane uphill until you come to a track on your left with a signpost reading: "This way to the waterfalls." Turn left here to follow **Stock Ghyll** upstream. Red waymarkers indicate the way to **Stockghyll Force**—do not cross the beck.

The path climbs steadily through a gorgeous area of woodland. A luxurious growth of mosses and lichens covers every possible surface—boulders, tree trunks, branches. These primitive plants don't have roots; they take in water and the nutrients they need to survive through their leaves and stems. The woodland in the gorge is a delight at any time of the year, but it is particularly colourful in spring when the ground is carpeted with daffodils.

At the highest viewpoint, you reach a junction of paths with a sign pointing the way to a revolving gate. Ignore the path to the right for now, although

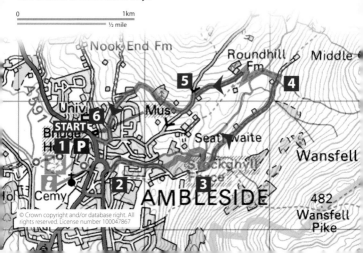

Movement and light: *A curtain of white water below Stockghyll Force*

you will come back to this point later. Continue uphill to the bridge over the top of the falls for an exciting sense of the volume of water crashing through this narrow gap.

For a closer view of the falls themselves, cross the bridge and head downstream until you see a railed path on the left in a few metres. This leads to the base of the higher section of the falls. The railings suddenly end here, so this path isn't suitable for dogs or young children.

3. Return to the junction with the 'Revolving Gate' sign, and bear left. Go through the wooden gate next to the old turnstile. A narrow path leads to a surfaced lane along which you turn left.

As you climb gently, soon crossing a cattle grid, the views open out; the ridge that can be seen up to the left leads on to **Red Screes**.

4. After around a kilometre of road walking, you will pass the entrance to **Low Grove House** on your left and cross a cattle grid. Immediately after this, turn left down a path that drops

Copper and gold: *The rich colours of fallen leaves illuminate the beck*

to a gate and then a bridge over **Stock Ghyll**. Swing left after the bridge, along a faint, grassy path that heads downstream alongside the beck for a short while. It then makes its way towards a gate in a wall. Don't go through the gate; instead, follow the stony path that swings up the hill to the right. It then loops left and goes through a small gate close to **Roundhill Farm**.

5. Turn left along the farm track. Turn left at the road and walk downhill for 200 metres. At a bend, take the rough track

on the right, going through a wooden gate set back from the road. After another gate, ignore the track uphill to the right; your route follows the wall on the left. Go through a small, gated stile and then bear left to walk downhill with a fence and a small plantation on your left. A tiny bridge over an equally tiny beck is then followed by another gated stile.

6. This leads on to a clear track on the **edge of Ambleside**. Follow this to a quiet road, along which you turn left. Swing left again at the postbox in the wall and follow the road downhill. Turn right at the T-junction opposite

Chapel Cottage. There is no pavement along this section of narrow road, so be particularly careful on the bends. It swings right—down **Smithy Brow** and past the **Golden Rule pub** on the left—to drop to a mini-roundabout. The pedestrian bridge into the car park is just to the left on the other side of the main road. ♦

Victorian spectacle

Stockghyll Force was popular with travellers at the end of the 19th century. With a refreshment shelter nearby, they passed through the turnstile at the top of the gorge, paying a penny to see the falls from the specially installed viewing platforms, bridges and benches. The hardiest visitors would even don bathing suits and take a dip in the bracing waters of the beck.

Scale Force, upper falls

Scale Force

Spectacular mountain scenery, two beautiful lakes and the Lake District's longest waterfall

What to expect:
Good paths near Buttermere, but then open, often boggy ground

Distance/time: 6km/ 4½ miles. Allow 2½-3 hours

Start: Lake District National Park pay and display car park behind Bridge Hotel, Buttermere

Grid ref: NY 174 169

Ordnance Survey Map: OL 4 *The English Lakes North-western area. Keswick, Cockermouth & Wigton*

After the walk: Croft House Café, Bridge Hotel and Fish Inn, all in Buttermere

Walk outline

The walk starts with a stroll alongside gorgeous Buttermere, surrounded by high, craggy mountains. A clear bridleway is then followed alongside Buttermere Dubs before the route begins climbing. The excellent views across Crummock Water make up for the damp, temporarily pathless ground crossed on the way to the waterfall. The return route is initially rough in places, but then regains good, clear paths.

Scale Force

The Lake District's longest waterfall, Scale Force, is located in a dark, damp and narrow ravine on the northern slopes of Red Pike and Starling Dodd. It looks fairly impressive from the slopes of neighbouring Melbreak to the north, but it is really only as you stand at its very base and crane your neck to gaze up at it that you get any sense of the immense height that is lost in just a short distance. The main drop, slender and surprisingly elegant, falls a tremendous thirty-eight metres. Add on the other, smaller falls and it totals about fifty-two metres. A truly awesome sight!

Sourmilk Gill

Gorse

The Walk

1. Leave the car park, head back out on to the road and turn right. Almost immediately, turn right along the farm lane—signposted 'Lakeshore path'. Go through two gates in quick succession as you head away from the buildings.

You soon catch glimpses of the waters of Buttermere below, and, over to the right, Sourmilk Gill cuts through the dark woods on the north-eastern slopes of Red Pike, plummeting more than 350 metres in less than one kilometre.

On reaching a large gate straight ahead,

Buttermere Dubs: *A shallow, crystal clear stream flows from Buttermere*

go through the smaller gate on the right. A second gate leads to a series of steps and then the path swings left. Beyond another gate, it passes through some trees and drops closer to the lakeshore.

2. Ignore the kissing-gate straight ahead; instead, turn right to drop to a gate providing access to a permitted footpath along the **shingle beach**. Head right along the shore and after the next gate, ignore the path to the right;

keep to the lakeshore route. This then swings right to a T-junction. Turn left to cross the footbridge over **Buttermere Dubs**.

3. Just before the next bridge, swing right to go through a kissing-gate close to **Sourmilk Gill**. Turn right—away from the bridge over the base of the gill. A stony path keeps close to the bottom of a steep, wooded slope. Having walked about 600 metres from Sourmilk Gill, you will see a humpback bridge on the right. Ignore this for now, but bear it in mind for later because it forms part of your return route. You cross one wooden footbridge over **Near Ruddy Beck** and then, as the path becomes less distinct, a second one over **Far Ruddy Beck**.

4. Parting company with the bridleway here, turn left to head upstream. After a few metres, you gain a reasonably clear

path going off to the right. Gradually gaining height, you are soon treated to views of **Crummock Water** down to the right and of **Mellbreak** straight ahead. The path isn't always clear, particularly as it crosses a flat, boggy area. After this though, it swings left to resume climbing and gains more solid ground. Apart from one last boggy patch, a good path now leads all the way to **Scale Force**.

5. After going through a kissing-gate, keep right at a fork to drop to the bridge over **Scale Beck**.

A trail on the left just before the bridge leads into the increasingly narrow ravine for a superb view of the waterfall. It takes you right to the base of the lower section of the falls, but you'll need to crane your neck to get a good view of the higher fall.

Across the lake: *Looking towards Scale Force, Red Pike and High Stile from the far side of Crummock Water*

To continue on the walk, cross the bridge, climb out of the gully and turn right—through a small gate. A clear path leads downhill beside **Scale Beck** and to a footbridge over **Black Beck**. Once over this, turn right along a narrow beckside path. Keep to the right of a dilapidated fence, tackling some damp ground as you continue downstream.

6. Cross the next bridge over **Black Beck**. Aim for the gap in the wall diagonally opposite to the left. Go through the gate and follow the path to another bridge. Once over this, the way ahead is less distinct again: swing half-left and you will pick up a faint, grassy path heading in the general direction of **Crummock Water**. This can be boggy in places, but eventually it drops on to a better, stony path.

You may recognise the next bridge you cross: this is where you left the bridleway earlier in the walk, just before the route began climbing. Swing half-right to pick up the path at the base of the steep slopes, briefly retracing your steps and crossing a second wooden bridge in a short while.

7. Watch for the **stone humpback**

bridge across **Buttermere Dubs** that you saw on the way out. Turn left to cross this. The track swings right and then left. Follow it to its junction with an even wider track, along which you turn left. This soon swings right—heading back into **Buttermere**. The entrance to the car park is just after the **Fish Inn** on your left. ♦

Sessile oaks

Much of the woodland between Sourmilk Gill and Far Ruddy Beck consists of native sessile oak. These oaks, with their stalkless acorns, are typical of upland areas with high rainfall, particularly in the north and west of Britain. Like their lowland cousin, the pedunculate oak, they can live for hundreds of years. But don't expect grand old, towering trees; the ancient oaks in the Lake District are often small and twisted.

The lower Holme Force cascade

Holme Force

An ancient 'corpse road' high above Loweswater and woodland paths lead to a secret waterfall

What to expect:

Woodland trails, track and farm paths; short, moderate climb

Distance/time: 8km/ 5 miles (including detour). Allow 3-3½ hours

Start: Maggie's Bridge car park near Loweswater, about half a mile west of the Kirkstile Inn

Grid ref: NY134 210

Ordnance Survey Map: OL 4 *The English Lakes North-western area. Keswick, Cockermouth & Wigton*

After the walk: Kirkstile Inn, Loweswater

Walk outline

A farm lane leads into Holme Wood where the climb begins. Emerging from the trees, the walk then joins the old 'corpse road'—a clear track with superb views of Loweswater and the surrounding fells. Following well signposted farm paths to the shores of Loweswater, it re-enters the National Trust-owned woodland, where a quick detour leads to Holme Force.

Holme Force

The delightful mixed woodland of Holme Wood cloaks the south-western shore of Loweswater, climbing to a high point of about 300 metres. Hidden away in the heart of the woods, seeing few visitors other than deer and red squirrels, is Holme Force. A succession of falls culminates in a narrow ribbon of water that runs down a smooth-sided chute and then tumbles over the boulder-strewn bed of Holme Beck. This is the prettiest and most easily accessible section of the falls, clearly visible from the track, but higher still are other cascades, including one which shoots off over the lip of the bedrock and forms a graceful mid-air arc.

Arc of spray

Wood anemones

The Walk

1. Go through the small gate next to the cattle grid and follow the track towards the lake and **Watergate Farm**. The track goes through the farmyard and swings right.

2. As soon as you go through the gate into **Holme Wood**, turn left to begin climbing on a narrower path. This crosses several old forest tracks as it ascends at a moderate angle.

3. Go through the kissing-gate at the edge of the woods and bear right, quickly joining a good track. This lovely, grassy route drops down to cross **Holme Beck** and then continues its undulating way around the side of **Burnbank Fell**.

From the beginning of the 13th century until the 17th century, when Loweswater was a chapel to St Bees Abbey, coffins would be carried on horseback along this bridleway to Lamplugh and then on to St Bees on the coast for burial. Despite its morbid beginnings, it's a delightful path and it has the added benefit of a well-placed bench a little way beyond Holme Beck; this affords some wonderful views down Loweswater and the northern end of Crummock Water, towered over by dramatic Grasmoor.

Beyond the bench, climb gently to the first of several gates—this one with a ladder stile beside it. Beyond the stile/gate, the track begins heading gently downhill.

Straight ahead, you can see Criffel on the other side of the Solway Firth. The eagle-eyed will also be able to make out the white masts of the Robin Rigg offshore wind farm.

Quiet waters: *Morning light, Loweswater*

4. About one kilometre from the first gate/stile, the track swings sharp left. Turn right here to cross a ladder stile near a fingerpost indicating that this is the way to 'Loweswater via Hudson Place'. Keep close to the wall on the right and the grassy path soon becomes more track-like as it descends. At a junction with a surfaced lane, turn right and then right again near the grey cottages at **Jenkinson Place**.

After crossing a stile by a gate, follow the faint but broad, grassy path half-left and through a gate. You then walk with a row of gnarled trees and bushes on your left. Cross a double stile at another gate and head towards Hudson Place. Just before the buildings, go through the gate on your left. Now keep close to the fence on the right, following the clear path to the next gate.

5. Once through this gate, turn right along the lane, soon passing in front of the buildings of **Hudson Place**. Two gates mark the end of the lane just after the farmhouse; go through the left-hand one, which looks straight down onto shimmering **Loweswater**.

High point: *Looking across to the fells above Loweswater and Crummock Water from the corpse road*

At the bottom of this path, cross the gate/stile to access the lakeshore track. Before long, this re-enters **Holme Wood**. Keep to the track; don't be tempted by the path to the left.

6. To make a short, extremely worthwhile detour to **Holme Force**, turn right along a less well used track about 300 metres after entering the woods. You will hear the waterfalls long before you see them. The main drop is located just above the bridge over **Holme Beck**,

but more adventurous walkers can cross the bridge and then turn right up a steep, narrow trail that provides views of the higher cascades. Seeing little sunlight, the ground here is often damp and slippery, and the exposed rock is slimy with moss, so watch your footing.

Returning to the point at which you left the main track (number **6** on the map), turn right. You soon cross a bridge and then pass a small building next to the lake—**Holme Bothy**.

This stone-built bothy was once a fish hatchery hut. Like the woods, the farm and the lake itself, it is now owned by the National Trust—and can be rented by

small groups. The facilities are simple: a cold water tap, wood-burning stove, four-ring gas cooker, composting toilet and a wooden platform on which to unroll your sleeping bag. But what a location!

Continue to the gate at the edge of the woods and then retrace your steps—through the yard of **Watergate Farm** and back to the car park. ◆

Red squirrels

Visitors to Holme Wood may be lucky enough to see red squirrels, a species that has been replaced in most of England and Wales by its grey cousin, introduced from North America in 1876. Partly because greys breed more rapidly and their extra body fat makes them better able to survive severe winters, they out-compete the reds, particularly in lowland deciduous woods. Red squirrels are also more susceptible to certain diseases.

Lodore Falls

Lodore Falls

*A wonderfully varied, picturesque walk exploring
Borrowdale's beautiful woodland and waterfalls*

What to expect:
*Low fells, woodland
and lakeside; mostly
clear paths; some road
walking*

Distance/time: 7km/ 4¼ miles. Allow 2½-3 hours

Start: Ashness Bridge car park

Grid ref: NY 269 196

Ordnance Survey Map: OL 4 *The English Lakes North-western area.
Keswick, Cockermouth & Wigton*

After the walk: The Lodore Falls Hotel and the Borrowdale Hotel
are open all day to non-residents

Walk outline

*Starting high above Derwentwater, with magnificent views
across the water, the walk slowly drops to the lakeshore for a
gentle stroll before making a detour to the Lodore Falls. The
only significant climb of the day comes after a short section of
road walking. This leads into oak woods beside Watendlath
Beck. The return, along a quiet lane, features a 'surprise view'.*

Lodore Falls

Hidden away in a dark, rocky, tree-shrouded ravine above
the Borrowdale road is a series of cascades known as the
Lodore Falls. The Romantic poets loved to wax lyrical about
Lakeland waterfalls, and this one is no exception. Robert
Southey wrote a strangely un-Romantic poem about the
falls 'thumping and plumping and bumping and jumping
and hissing and whizzing'. His colleague Samuel Taylor
Coleridge described it as 'beyond all rivalry the first and
best thing of the whole Lake Country'. If you visit during a
dry summer, you might wonder what all the fuss is about;
but see it after heavy rain, and there's no doubting its
magnificence.

Lodore jetty

Cuckoo

The Walk

1. Turn left out of the car park and walk down the road. Soon after crossing **Ashness Bridge**, probably the most photographed bridge in the whole of the Lake District, watch for a squat fingerpost to the right of the road. Take the narrow footpath here: it briefly runs parallel with the road, but then swings up to a gate in a wall. With Skiddaw straight ahead and superb views across to Cat Bells, keep to the clear path heading gently downhill.

2. Roughly 700 metres along this path, you reach a small, open, grassy area with a crag up to the right. Turn sharp left here, almost back on yourself. A low signpost beside the path indicates this is the way to the 'Borrowdale Road'. Descending through the trees, the stony path drops to the **Watendlath road**, along which you turn right.

3. At the T-junction, go through the tiny gap in the wall opposite to access the **Derwentwater lakeshore** close to a wooden jetty. (If the water level is high, you will have to turn left along the road to reach the Kettlewell car park.) Turn left along the stony beach, soon going through a gate in a fence.

On a calm day, Derwentwater is a photographer's dream, with the fells on the other side of the lake, notably Cat Bells, perfectly reflected in the water. If you look to the north, Skiddaw too makes a wonderful backdrop to this serene scene.

The trail heads back inland and then, after going through another gate, makes use of a causeway-like path just below the level of the road to reach the

Picturesque bridge: *The famous view of Skiddaw from Ashness Bridge*

National Trust's **Kettlewell car park**. The lakeshore path ends here: cross the road and go through the gap in the wall opposite to pick up a path continuing in the same direction through the woods.

Birdsong fills the trees; and, if you're visiting during the spring, you may even be lucky enough to hear the Borrowdale cuckoo.

When the path forks at a white waymarker, bear left. Before long, you reach a junction of paths behind the **Lodore Falls Hotel**. The main route

goes right here, but turn left for a five-minute detour to the **Lodore Falls** themselves.

Back on the main route cross the small bridge at the back of the hotel and go through its rear car park.

4. On reaching the road, cross over, turn left and walk beside the road.

5. In about 700 metres, go through the gate on the left just after **High Lodore Farm**—it has a fingerpost beside it. The path bends to the left, goes through a gate behind the farmhouse and then swings right. As it starts climbing more steeply, ignore the climbers' path off to

What a picture!: *Derwentwater, Cat Bells and distant Skiddaw from the Surprise View*

the left; simply keep to the zig-zags as they make their way past a bench and steadily up the hillside.

Just before reaching a wall at the top of the climb, bear right to pass through a gap in the wall. You soon go through a small gate above another waterfall on **Watendlath Beck**.

The path through the gorgeous oak woods is usually easy to follow, but leaf litter can sometimes obscure it. Make sure you keep right at anything that looks like a fork. Before long, you climb

through a shallow gully between two knolls and then reach a gate in a wall. Go through and turn left, soon crossing the footbridge over **Watendlath Beck**.

6. The path then goes back through the wall on your left. A clear track leads through these woods to a minor road, along which you turn left. The car park where the walk started is little more than one kilometre down this road, but, as you draw level with a small parking area on the way, there's a pleasant surprise...

Surprise View *is a wonderfully dramatic spot, partially concealed from the road by trees. But step off the asphalt and the*

ground suddenly drops away at your feet, revealing a flawless panorama which embraces Cat Bells, Maiden Moor, Skiddaw, Derwentwater and even Bassenthwaite Lake. Inevitably, on a clear day, there will be photographers standing with cameras and tripods at the ready—as at Ashness Bridge. ◆

Hanging valley

Watendlath Beck is one of the Lake District's many hanging valleys—a product of the last Ice Age. 'Hanging' above the level of the glaciated valley floor of Borrowdale, it was gouged out by a tributary to the main glacier, and so didn't erode as deeply. The difference in levels is exaggerated, too, by the Skiddaw slates of the main valley eroding more quickly than the Borrowdale volcanics, on which the beck lies.

Aira Force, above Ullswater

Aira Force

Through an arboretum to spectacular waterfalls and on to a low fell with breathtaking views

What to expect:
Clear paths, rough in places; low-lying fell

Distance/time: 6.5km/ 4 miles. Allow 2½-3 hours

Start: National Trust pay and display car park at Aira Force on A592, 2½ miles north-east of Glenridding

Grid ref: NY 400 200

Ordnance Survey Map: OL 5 *The English Lakes North-eastern area. Penrith, Patterdale & Caldbeck*

After the walk: Small café next to car park or choice of pubs and cafés in nearby Glenridding

Walk outline

Good paths lead through a wide and often exotic variety of trees to spectacular Aira Force. The route becomes a little rougher as it continues upstream, past High Force. Turning off on to what is, at first, a less well defined path, it then climbs at a moderate angle on to Gowbarrow Fell to complete a circuit of the top of the fell.

Aira Force and High Force

As Aira Beck flows from the northernmost hills of the Helvellyn range, it gradually gathers volume and momentum on its journey to Ullswater. The first of the falls it forms as it enters the Aira gorge is High Force, a series of dramatic cascades. Losing height at an ever increasing rate, it then thunders downstream in a whirling torrent until, finally, it reaches its crescendo and plummets a massive twenty-one metres to form Aira Force, one of the most stunning waterfalls in the Lake District. At the foot of this tremendous drop are sheer-sided pools, and, all around, trees cling to the edges of the ravine. It's a magnificent, even daunting sight.

Gowbarrow Fell summit

Jay

The Walk

1. At the far end of the car park, go through the gap in the stone construction. Like the gateway in the children's classic *The Secret Garden*, this gap holds the key to a number of surprises. Having passed through a couple of gates and crossed a tiny beck, you reach an area of **ancient yews and towering conifers**.

Turn left here, away from the iron railings on the right, to slowly ascend, with the beck on your right, to a bench.

Turn right to descend the steep stone staircase to the base of powerful **Aira Force**, feeling the spray from the falls on your face.

The drama of this setting has inspired many writers, and the poet William Wordsworth, who was a frequent visitor to the area, wrote no fewer than three poems about Aira Force. The most well known of these is The Somnambulist. *This tells the local legend of two lovers who were parted by war. As the knight went off to fight, his sweetheart was left at home, worrying about him. Her anxiety led her to start sleepwalking along the edge of the steep Aira gorge. When the knight returned, he discovered her asleep and in this precarious position. He touched her and she awoke, lost her balance and fell to her death.*

2. Cross the bridge at the bottom of the falls and turn left immediately—up another steep, stone stairway, to join a path coming in from the right. Here, a brief detour to the left takes walkers on to the stone

0   1km

½ mile

Stunning panorama: *The northern end of Ullswater from the summit of Gowbarrow Fell*

humpback bridge at the top of the noisy falls.

Back on the main path, there is quite a bit of clambering to be done as you wend your way upstream. In a couple of hundred metres, you will see a path branching left to a wooden footbridge below. Ignore this, and continue, with the beck on your left, past **High Force.** The trees thin out after you pass through a gap in a wall and then disappear entirely beyond a gate.

3. Just before another gate—a small, wooden gate beside a larger farm gate—turn right to start climbing on a faint path. Cross the ladder stile and head steeply uphill with the wall on your left. After 700 metres of uphill slog, the path finally levels off slightly and swings right—away from the wall—towards the Ordnance Survey 'trig' point on the summit of **Gowbarrow Fell**.

4. Descend north-east at first, then follow the clear path round to the remains of an **old shooting hut** on the eastern edge of the fell.

Lake and fells: *Gowbarrow Fell enjoys superb views across Ullswater to Place Fell and the Helvellyn range*

5. Bear right here. Around one kilometre beyond the ruin, you round the side of a crag and are suddenly met by arguably the most **magnificent panorama** in the eastern Lakes.

Breathtaking is an over-used adjective, but, on this occasion, it is hard to resist that sharp intake of breath as the western expanse of Ullswater is revealed with the dark, craggy Helvellyn range in the background. This is a place to linger—and, conveniently, there is a bench nearby.

The level path then continues for a short while before dropping gently to a fence.

*As you descend, you will see what looks like a medieval tower below. This is **Lyulph's Tower** and isn't as old as it looks; it was built as a shooting lodge in 1780.*

6. Once through the gate, bear left at the next junction to descend through the woods to cross a bridge over **Aira Beck**. Climb the steps on the other side and bear left through a gap in some iron railings to return to the car park.

Many of the trees in the arboretum around Aira Force were planted by the Howard family of Greystoke. They were lords of

the manor here from the late Middle Ages until they sold the land to the National Trust in 1906. The fine specimens include a Douglas fir that is said to be the tallest tree in Cumbria, some ancient yews and a Chilean pine or 'Monkey Puzzle' tree. There are also two huge sitka spruces on the eastern side of the beck, dating back to 1846. The largest has a girth of more than six metres. ♦

Wild daffodils

The woods below Gowbarrow are said to have inspired Wordsworth to write his most famous poem, Daffodils. Having walked there with him in April 1802, his sister Dorothy noted in her diary: "I never saw daffodils so beautiful..." Two years later, he used her subsequent observations as the basis of a poem, the first line of which is probably the most famous in English poetry: "I wandered lonely as a cloud..."

White water at the Howk

The Howk

A walk through a dark, atmospheric limestone gorge, home to a ruined mill and a waterfall

What to expect:
Riverside trail, farm paths and some quiet lanes

Distance/time: 5km/ 3 miles. Allow 1½-2 hours

Start: Free Lake District National Park Authority car park in Caldbeck

Grid ref: NY 323 398

Ordnance Survey Map: OL 5 *The English Lakes North-eastern area. Penrith, Patterdale & Caldbeck*

After the walk: The Oddfellows Arms pub, the Old Smithy café and the Watermill restaurant (Priest's Mill), all in Caldbeck

Walk outline

An easy riverside stroll leads past a ruined bobbin mill, up to the waterfalls of The Howk and into the countryside beyond. Using quiet lanes and an old, grassy farm track, the walk then climbs towards the base of the lonely Northern Fells before dropping back down into Caldbeck. This gorgeous conservation village is also well worth exploring if you have time to spare.

The Howk

'A delicious spot in which to breathe out a summer's day— limestone rocks, hanging trees, pools and waterbreaks— caves and cauldrons which have been honoured with fairy names....' So wrote Dorothy Wordsworth after visiting The Howk in 1803 with her brother William and their friend Coleridge. And 'delicious' it is: a deafening set of falls that spirals down through a cool, narrow, ravine that is home to dense vegetation, including the rare shield fern. The rock here is limestone—unusual in the Lake District—resulting in the 'caves and cauldrons' Dorothy observed, many of which are now fenced off for safety reasons.

Caldbeck Church

Shield fern

The Walk

1. Leave the car park through the vehicle exit (not the entrance) and turn left. Within 50 metres, as the lane swings left, go through the gate on the right—surprisingly, through someone's front yard. Once through the next gate, a track leads to some interesting ruins.

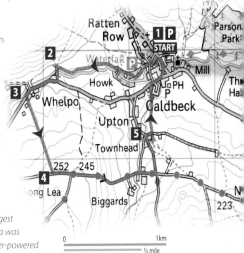

Howk bobbin mill, built in 1857, used to have a 42 foot waterwheel, said to be the largest of its kind in England. Cumbria was once home to about 120 water-powered bobbin mills.

Beyond the mill, climb beside **The Howk waterfall** and then, ignoring a bridge, continue upstream. Just after a small gate, the now less distinct path crosses open ground. Keep close to the water and then go through two small gates in quick succession.

2. Just over a kilometre beyond Caldbeck, cross the bridge on your left over **Whelpo Beck**. Head to the left of the buildings at Beckstones, and you will find a stile to the left of the garden wall. Turn right along the road, and follow it round to the left through **Whelpo**.

3. Just after the last house, go through the gate on the left. Follow the track to the right of the farm sheds. It narrows as it heads steadily uphill; the final section is just a fenced strip of grass between fields.

4. Turn left at the road. Up to the right, the northernmost Lakeland fells are visible, including High Pike. Straight ahead, the North Pennines appear as a misty outline on the horizon. The road drops to the buildings at **Wath**. Ignore the turning on the left for Caldbeck. Continue for another 200 metres and then turn left along a track.

Water power: *Howk bobbin mill once made wooden reels for the local textile industry*

5. This comes out on to a road. Almost immediately, turn right along another track. In 60 metres, go through the kissing-gate up to the left. Keep close to the field boundary on your left, but when the fence bends left, keep straight ahead, making for the gates below.

These provide access to a small area of woodland. The clear path crosses a bridge and ends at a gate. Once through this, turn left and immediately right to join the main road through **Caldbeck**. Turn left—towards Carlisle and past the **Old Smithy**. The car park is ahead on the left. ♦

D'ye Ken John Peel?

Caldbeck's church is the resting place of 19th-century huntsman John Peel, immortalised in the song D'ye Ken John Peel? Peel led a self-indulgent life; his wife owned enough land to provide them with a comfortable income without him having to work. His close friend John Woodcock Graves admitted hunting dominated his life: 'I believe he would not have left the drag of a fox on the impending death of a child.'

Useful Information

Cumbria Tourism

Cumbria Tourism's official website covers everything from accommodation and events to attractions and adventure. **www.golakes.co.uk**

Lake District National Park

The Lake District National Park website also has information on things to see and do, plus maps, webcams and news. **www.lakedistrict.gov.uk**

Tourist Information Centres

The main TICs provide free information on everything from accommodation and travel to what's on and walking advice.

Ambleside	01539 432 582	tic@thehubofambleside.com
Bowness	01539 442 895	bownesstic@lake-district.gov.uk
Coniston	01539 441 533	mail@conistontic.org
Keswick	01768 772 645	keswicktic@lake-district.gov.uk
Penrith	01768 867 466	pen.tic@eden.gov.uk
Ullswater	01768 482 414	ullswatertic@lake-district.gov.uk
Windermere	01539 446 499	windermeretic@southlakeland.gov.uk

Emergencies

The Lake District is covered by twelve volunteer mountain rescue teams. In a real emergency:

1. Make a note of your location (with OS grid reference, if possible); the name, age and sex of the casualty; their injuries; how many people are in the group; and your mobile phone number.

2. Dial 999 or 112 and ask for the Cumbria police, and then for Mountain Rescue.

3. Give them your prepared details.

4. Do NOT change position until contacted by the mountain rescue team.

Weather

Five day forecast for the Lake District

0844 846 2444   **www.lakedistrict.gov.uk/weatherline**